The Whizzkid's Handbook

This book belongs to

. . . .

. . . .

. . . .

WHIZZ KID

Other books by Peter Eldin in Armada

THE TRICKSTER'S HANDBOOK
THE SECRET AGENT'S HANDBOOK
THE EXPLORER'S HANDBOOK
THE NEW ARMADA TV QUIZ BOOK
TOP OF THE POPS QUIZ
ISN'T THAT AMAZING!

Peter Eldin

The Whizzkid's Handbook

with drawings by Roger Smith

An Armada Original

The Whizzkid's Handbook was first published in
Armada in 1979 by Fontana Paperbacks,
14 St James's Place, London SW1A 1PS

This impression 1980

© Eldin Editorial Services

Printed in Great Britain by Love & Malcomson
Ltd., Brighton Road, Redhill, Surrey.

Contents

WARNING

THIS BOOK IS UNSUITABLE
FOR
TEACHERS
OR
ADULTS OF NERVOUS
DISPOSITION

Foreword

At long last here is the book that every schoolboy and schoolgirl has been waiting for—an invaluable guide on how to survive school.

Teachers have to be trained to do their job, but no one thinks to train the pupil. For ten or more long years of his life the poor pupil is left to his own devices, to struggle through school as best he can with little help, encouragement, or advice.

Now that advice is available! The concentrated wisdom of pupils throughout the ages has been gathered together in one volume to provide an indispensable guide for all scholars. Most of the information contained in this book has been handed down from pupil to pupil for countless generations by word of mouth or by paper pellets thrown across the room, and is now revealed for the benefit of all schoolkids for the first time . . .

An indispensable guide for all scholars..

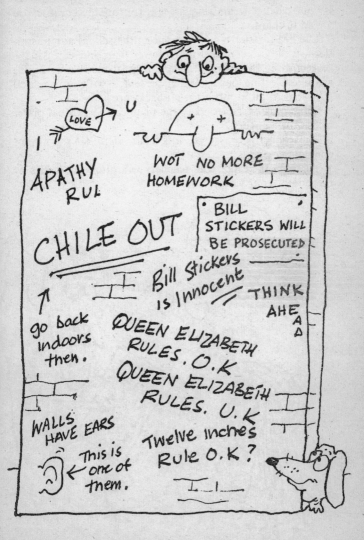

Guide to Teachers and Their Habits

If your teacher wears sunglasses it is probably because you are so brilliant.

The headmaster is number one in the school administration—well, you can't get much lower than one, can you?

According to several teachers, a great number of pupils are like blotting paper. When presented with information they soak it all in but get it all backwards.

Some music teachers play the piano by ear. (Most prefer to use their fingers.)

If a teacher is cross-eyed it is a sure sign that she cannot control her pupils.

To show they like you, teachers will often put a kiss by the side of your work.

Excuses for Bad Reports

If you get a bad school report, here are some things you can say to your dad to delay that inevitable moment when he discovers that you are a lazy, good-for-nothing idler.

"I think the teacher has put the wrong name on the report." (This is especially good if you receive your report on a Friday as your dad will not be able to check up on you until Monday, which gives you a couple of days' respite. If you receive your school report at the end of term it is even better for it will be several weeks before he can do anything —and he may have forgotten all about it by then.)

"I've had excellent marks all through the term. It is just that the teachers don't like me because I am so clever."

"Einstein always got bad school reports."

"I don't understand the teachers."

"The teachers don't understand me."

"Oh, dear! I lost my school report on the way home and I did so want you to see how well I have been doing."

"Don't take any notice of it. The teachers have written exactly the same about everyone in the class."

"Goodbye, I'm leaving home."

school report

Flogmore School
great wackingham, herts.

NAME **NOAH LITTLE**   CLASS **B4.T**

ARITHMETIC	I don't know what makes Noah so stupid but whatever it is — it works
GEOGRAPHY	He and his friend never get less than 98% in exams. His friend gets 90% and Noah gets 8%.
ENGLISH	His essays are bad in only three places - the beginning, the middle, and the end.
FRENCH	Noah is as smart as the next boy. The only trouble is that the next boy is an idiot.
BIOLOGY	Good news! Noah has been awarded a place in medical school - but they don't want him while he's still alive.

MUSIC	When Noah plays Chopin, Chopin loses. But his singing is improving. People are putting cotton wool in only one ear now.
ART	Noah suffers from art failure ~ he ought to have a transplant.
SPORT	We call Noah "DAISY" Some days 'e runs and some days 'e doesn't.
WOODWORK	The things Noah has made in woodwork are all good for something – burning.

FORM MASTER   Noah is so stupid he even sits at the back of the school bus because he thinks he gets a longer ride

I. Thumpem.

HEADMASTER

Noah knows all the answers. It's just the questions that confuse him

I. Thumpem-Harder.

On The Right Lines

One of the first things teachers learn at teachers' training college is that children hate doing lines. No matter how careful you are, it is very difficult to get through the whole of one's school life without doing lines. There are, however, several ways of making the task of writing lines a lot easier.

Teachers' training college.

1. **Instant Lines** Write out the line ten times. *"I must not throw pellets at the teacher"*, or whatever it is that you must write. Now ask your sister's boyfriend to take the sheet of paper to his office and to photocopy it ten times. In that way you will have a hundred lines, which is usually the number teachers ask for. (If your sister's boyfriend refuses to do this little favour for you, tell him that you will tell your sister that you have seen him out with another girl—that should get him worried.)

2. **Quadruple Lines** Another good way to make the writing of lines much easier is to tape a number of pencils together as shown in the illustration. This is a great labour-saving idea for it enables you to write a number of lines all at the same time. If you have lines regularly you may find it worthwhile to make the more elaborate device demonstrated by our hero on the cover of this book.

3. Family Lines If you have got a little brother (or sister) who can write neatly, and whom you can bribe with pocket money, chocolate, marbles, etc, get him to write out the lines for you.

4. Downright Dangerous, Double-quick Lines This scheme is only for úse by the experienced pupil for it takes a bit of nerve to carry off. It is a well-known fact that although teachers like giving out lines they do not like reading them. Usually they are so pleased that you have suffered and missed your favourite television programme that they only glance through the papers and do not actually bother to read the lines.

All you have to do, therefore, is to write out the top and bottom sheets. On the sheets in between all you do is scribble. (Some teachers are wise to this so be careful who you try it on.)

17

Daft Definitions

These definitions will not help you to shine in English—but your trousers might shine from the canings you could receive if you use them in a lesson!

ASSET—a baby donkey

AUTONOMY—the history of motor cars

BACTERIA—the rear door of a self-service cafe

BIPLANE—what the pilot says as he jumps out

BLOTTING PAPER—something you look for while the ink dries

CINNAMON—a Scots film actor

CIRCLE—a round line with no kinks in it joined up neatly so you can't tell where it started

CIRCUMFERENCE—a knight of the Round Table

COLLISION—what happens when two motorists go after the same pedestrian

CONFIDENCE—the feeling people have before they know better

CONJURING—telling lies with the fingers

COWARD—someone who wears water wings in the bath

DENIAL—a river in Egypt

DENTIST—someone who'll give you the drill of your life

DOCTOR—the only person that enjoys poor health

DUCK—a chicken on snow shoes

EARWIG—false hair that keeps your ears warm

FJORD—a Norwegian motor car

FOOTBALL—a game that uses one ball, twenty-two players, and several thousand referees

GLUTTON—anyone who beats you to the last piece of cake

IGLOO—toilet for Igs

INFANTRY—baby soldiers

JIGSAW PUZZLE—a pastime invented by a Scotsman who dropped a pound note in a mincer

LOGARITHMS—tunes played at a wood-cutters ball

MACADAM—the first Scotsman

MINIATURE—a dwarf eating a toffee

MONOPOLY—a parrot not equipped with stereo

MUSHROOM—school canteen

OCTOPUS—an eight-sided cat

OPTIMIST—a happychondriac

PARACHUTIST—someone who climbs down trees he never climbed up

PENICILLIN—just the thing to give someone who has everything

PERCH—a fish found in a bird cage

PHYSICS—the science of making lemonade and other fizzy drinks

POLYGON—an empty parrot cage

POSTMAN—someone who gets the sack every day he goes to work

RHUBARB—bloodshot celery

ROYALTY—what the Queen drinks

SCHOOL—a place where they teach you things you'll never need to know when you leave it

SCHOOL DESK—a wastepaper basket with a lid

SEA SHELL—ammunition used by a Navy gunboat

SLUG—a nude snail

SUCCEED—what a toothless budgie does

STAIRS—things that go up and down without moving

SOLVENT—air-conditioning for shoes

SNOWBALL—a snowman's dance

TOMORROW—something that is always coming but never arrives

VIOLIN—a bad hotel

Tips for Cookery Classes

The best thing to put into a jam roly poly is your teeth.

To keep your cookery classroom clear of flies, put a pile of horse manure in the dining room.

To make chicken go further, cross it with a centipede and then there will be enough legs to go round.

To carry two gallons of milk in a leather bag without spilling any—leave it in the cow.

To calculate the colour of plums use a green gauge.

The best way to prevent milk from going sour is to drink it.

Never throw banana skins away—they make good slippers.

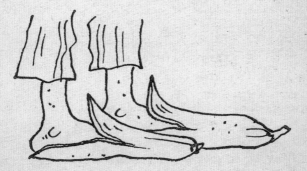

To make leek soup, just hold a saucepan below a hole in the ceiling when it's raining.

If you stay to school dinners you'll never live to regret it.

At one school when they run out of Brussels sprouts they paint mothballs green and pretend that they are Brussels. They don't taste very nice but they keep the moths out of your stomach.

Questions and Answers

Here are a few questions taken from examination papers, with the correct answers for you to study.

For what is Isaac Newton famous?
An apple fell on his head and he discovered the law of graffiti

What do you know about the great composers of the 18th century?
They are all dead

Who was Joan of Arc?
Noah's wife.

What famous composer had a piano with one leg missing?
Liszt

Why did the Spanish Armada fail?
Because it didn't do enough miles to the galleon

What is the similarity between an elephant and a hippopotamus?
Neither can play cricket

Who is the greatest English poet?
Anon—he wrote more poems than anyone else

Lesson Timetable

Ivor Grudge is a miserable schoolteacher who does everything he can to make life as difficult as possible for his pupils. He never gives them a straightforward lesson timetable but makes them work it out for themselves. Below is a typical Ivor Grudge timetable for a day. From the clues given, can you work out the order in which the lessons will be taken?

There are four lessons in the morning and four in the afternoon.

English is the first lesson after lunch.

Geography is before Arithmetic.

English is before French.

History comes between Physics and French.

Biology is between Geography and Chemistry.

The answer is on page 127.

A Note for All Reasons

For some reason best known to themselves, teachers do not trust kids. They always insist on receiving a note from your parents if you are off school for any reason. (Some teachers are so bad in this respect they even insist on their marriage partners bringing a note if they are down late for breakfast.)

To save parents the trouble of writing a note each time you are off school, have this all-purpose note photocopied at your local stationer so you will always have a supply available. All you have to do each time is simply cross out the words or phrases that do not apply. Just think of all that valuable time such a note will save your mum and dad!

Dear *(insert teacher's name)*

Little *(insert your name)*

was off school
yesterday
last week
last year
tomorrow
because

he
she
couldn't get out of bed.
had a brain failure.
was presented to the Queen.
is too clever for your silly lessons.

As a result
he
she
is still very
weak
lazy
stinky
and

should not do any
games
arithmetic
sock washing
thing
for the

next
two days.
fortnight.
year.
100 years.

Yours sincerely,

(insert parent's name)

School Dinners

If you stay to school dinners
Better throw them aside;
A lot of kids didn't,
A lot of kids died.

The meat is made of iron,
The spuds are made of steel;
And if that don't get you,
The afters will!

ANON

Dining Room Definitions

Dining room supervisors give food fancy names, but the following dictionary is given so that all schoolchildren can instantly identify whatever is put before them.

School Name	Actual Name
Beans on toast	skinheads on a raft
Cornflakes	dehydrated wheat
Semolina	wallpaper paste
Tapioca pudding	frog-spawn
Cabbage	seaweed
Irish stew	mudballs in swamp
Ravioli	soggy pillows
Treacle tart	glue on cardboard
Roast potatoes	conkers
Eccles cake	squashed flies
Cauliflower	bits of brain
Spaghetti bolognaise	worms in gravy
New boiled potatoes	cod's eyes
Sausages	U.F.O.s (Unidentified Frying Objects)
Bacon	*B*anic *A*nodide *C*hlorinate *O*f *N*itrate
Beefburgers and mash	shoe soles on cement
Steak and kidney	snake and pigmy
Milk shake	nervous cow
Faggots	meatballs of maggots
Hard-boiled eggs	Kojaks

People of the World

Some useless information about the people who live in different places around the world:

People who live in Paris are called Parasites
People who live in Moscow are called Mosques
People who live in Venice are called Venusians
People who live in Hamburg are called Hamburgers
People who live in Dublin are called Dubloons
People who live in Peking are called Peking Toms
People who live in Hong Kong are called Hong Konkers
People who live in Delhi are called Dahlias
People who live in Frankfurt are called Frankfurters
People who live in Munich are called Munchers
People who live in Naples are called Napoleons
People who live in Fiji are called Fidgets
People who live in Malta are called Maltesers
People who live in Sardinia are called Sardines

PRODUCE OF SARDINIA

Cock-eyed Countries

In a geography exam the pupils were asked to identify the shapes of certain countries and continents. The outlines given were those shown here. Can you identify them?

To make the problem a little more difficult they have been printed on their sides or upside-down, and they have not all been drawn to the same scale.

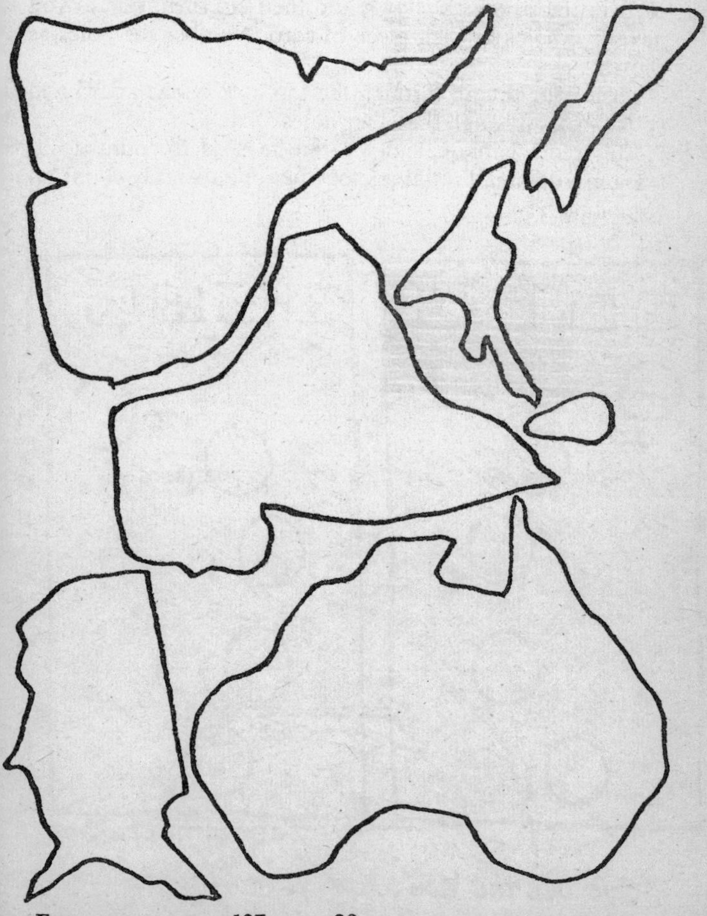

For answer see p. 127.   29

Cardboard Calculator

It is often useful to have a calculator handy during arithmetic lessons. Unfortunately, calculators can prove to be quite expensive but the Whizzkid's calculator shown here will cost you nothing at all.

You will need two pieces of cardboard each measuring about 7 centimetres by 12 centimetres. Make circles on each card in the positions shown and then cut them out so you have five holes in each piece of card. Number the holes as shown.

Push your thumb through the top hole of each card and your fingers through the other holes.

This remarkable calculator can be used to count up to ten and add small numbers together. You simply count on your fingers!

Cut out the holes for your fingers

To use the calculator to multiply small numbers, this is what you do: First you touch together the two fingers for the two numbers you wish to multiply. Now count them and all the fingers below them to give you the tens of your answer. Count the fingers above and multiply them together to get the units.

Let us take an example and you will see how easy it is. If, for example, you wish to multiply 8 by 9 just touch together the appropriate two fingers as indicated by the numbers you wrote on the cardboard calculator. Counting these two fingers and all the ones below gives you a total of seven. Above the eight finger are two fingers and above the nine finger is one. One times two equals two. Put this answer beside the tens number (7) and you have the answer 72, so 8 times 9 equals 72.

Try it with some other numbers and you will see that it works every time. It does not, however, work for the numbers one to five—you will have to learn your multiplication tables for them. Sorry about that!

Remember, Remember

Quite often it is necessary to remember a number of items for a test or an examination. There is no need to get worried by this type of question for it is very easy to remember a list of things, as you will see. A simple method of committing such a list to memory is given here. Once you have grasped the basic principle you will be able to use this method to remember quite long lists of things.

To explain how the method works, let us take as an example the eight reasons why elephants do not like tomato soup. (Well, that is no more crazy than some of the things you may be expected to remember.)

Elephants do not like tomato soup because:

1. it stains their trunks
2. tomato soup is not sold by their local supermarket (or should that be soupermarket?)
3. it reminds them of blood
4. they can't get the cans open
5. it is against their religion
6. it makes them see red
7. they prefer oxtail
8. they do not like the taste

To remember the various items in this or any other list, first go through and pick out a key word in each item. This is a word, or a couple of words, that give the whole item in a nutshell. For example, the key words in the list we are using are *trunks, supermarket, blood, cans, religion, red, oxtail,* and *taste.*

The next thing you have to do is to link the various items together in your mind so that the recollection of the first item will naturally lead on to the recollection of all the other items in the list. This is how you do it: First make a mental picture that incorporates the keywords for both the first and the second items (trunks/supermarket). This mental picture should be as exaggerated and as funny as you can make it, and it does not necessarily have to have any direct connection with the main subject matter. The sort of thing you might imagine for the first link is a picture of you standing in your local *supermarket* wearing only your swimming *trunks*.

As a test to see if this method works, do not just read this description but actually try to make the mental links as they are suggested. Imagine yourself in that busy supermarket wearing only your swimming costume. Everyone is staring and laughing at you. Just think how embarrassed you will be.

Having made this mental link, forget it—for the moment —and go on to make a similar mental link between items 2 and 3. In this case (*supermarket/blood*) you might imagine your local *supermarket* flowing with *blood*. There is blood everywhere—on the floors, on the shelves, and even seeping down the walls (ugh, this is worse than a horror movie). Alternatively, you might imagine yourself at the checkout filling your carrier bag with blood or, perhaps, paying your bill not with money but with—yes, you guessed it—blood.

33

B

It does not really matter what sort of mental picture you form as long as it helps you to remember, and, as you will find out if you follow this section right through to the end, this system will enable you to remember all manner of things.

Having mentally linked items 2 and 3, the next step is to link items 3 and 4, then 4 and 5, then 5 and 6, ... and so on.

Here are some suggested links for the rest of the reasons why elephants do not like tomato soup. Just for a bit of fun try to visualise the links suggested—you may find that you will learn something useful.

3-4 *blood, cans* imagine a factory in which cans are filled with blood or perhaps opening a can of peaches in the kitchen at home only to find it is full of blood.

4-5 *cans, religion* the picture you form here may depend upon which religious faith you follow. If Christian you might imagine a large cross made of tin cans.

34

5–6 *religion, red* form a picture of a church congregation all dressed in red clothes.

6–7 *red, oxtail* think of waving a red sheet at an ox with a large tail. To make the picture funny, so you will remember it easier, imagine the tail being larger than the ox.

7–8 *oxtail, taste* imagine yourself trying to taste an oxtail but it is still on the ox, which runs away pulling you along with it.

Once all the links have been made all you have to do is remember the first of the eight reasons why elephants do not like tomato soup (it stains their trunks). As soon as you do this you will find that the mention of the word *trunks* makes the first of your mental pictures spring to mind and immediately you know that the next word in the chain is *supermarket* (tomato soup is not sold by their local supermarket). This brings to mind *blood*, blood recalls cans, cans make you think of religion and so on through the list.

It really is quite easy isn't it?

If you did not try out the method as you read it, go back to the beginning of this section and make the mental links as suggested. In no time at all you will know the eight reasons why elephants do not like tomato soup.

You can do the same thing with any list of items you have to remember. Just try it and see. Very soon you will be getting better results in tests and examinations—you may even become top of the class . . !

Decision-Maker

If you wake up one morning on a lovely day and you cannot decide whether to go to the zoo, go fishing, or attend school, here is how you can make the decision more easily. Simply take a coin and let chance make the decision for you.

Toss the coin in the air.

If it comes down heads, go to the zoo. If it comes down tails, spend the day fishing. If it lands on its edge then go to school . . .

Problems in English

What is the longest word in the English language?

  Smiles (because there is a mile between the first and last letters)

Why is the letter T like an island?

  Because it is surrounded by waTer

When were there only three vowels?

  Before U and I were born

What English word is always spelt incorrectly?

  Incorrectly

What letter makes a quarter of a mile?

  M, I, L, or E

What is the longest word in the English language?

  Elastic (because it stretches)

Questions in Cookery

What stays hot when you put it in the fridge?
Mustard

How do you make a plum punch?
Teach it how to box

If you put your fingers in a glass of milk what have you made?
A hand-shake

How do you make a Swiss roll?
Push him over an Alp

The recipe reads "pick up the fruit and then place it on the table upside-down". What are you making?
Apple turnover

How do you make puffed wheat?
Chase it round the garden

If you invite a group of ghosts to dinner what should you give them to eat?
Ghoulash

Tebahpla

What is Tebahpla? It is *alphabet* spelled backwards. Most people can recite the alphabet but a Whizzkid can go one better. He or she can write it backwards.

It is of course possible to learn the letters of the alphabet in reverse. But to a Whizzkid that is too much bother. There must be an easier way—and there is.

All you have to do is learn a short poem. Once you know it you will find it is very easy to recite the alphabet backwards. It will certainly impress your friends and your teachers. Here is the poem with the letters of the alphabet above each word. The poem does not make sense but you will find that this doesn't matter. Just keep on learning it until you can recite the complete alphabet very fast backwards.

Z   Y   X   W   V
Said Wye, Eggs double you fee.

U T S R Q P
You tea is our Kew pea.

O N M L K J
Oh, en 'em 'ell K J,

I H GFE DC BA
I hate G if he deceive B.A.

40

Will It Divide Exactly?

To work out whether or not a number can be divided exactly may take some time. If you memorise the following rules you may find this process a lot easier.

Any number can be divided by 2 if its last digit is even.

      " 3 if the sum of its digits can be divided by 3.

      " 4 if its last *two* digits are divisible by 4.

      " 5 if it ends with a 0 or a 5.

      " 6 if the complete number can be divided by both 2 and 3.

      " 8 if the last *three* digits can be divided by 8.

      " 9 if the sum of its digits can be divided by 9.

      " 10 if it ends with a 0.

It's a Date

Remembering dates is often a problem. One way that a Whizzkid overcomes the problem is to make up a little rhyme including the date. Rhymes are quite easy to remember. Try making up some rhymes for yourself and you may become top of the class in history. Here are some examples to give you a start.

Columbus crossed the Atlantic in 1492
   In fourteen hundred and ninety-two
   Columbus sailed the ocean blue.

William IV died in 1837
   William the Fourth went to Heaven
   In eighteen hundred and thirty-seven.

Spanish Armada: 1588
   The Spanish Armada? It's special date,
   Is fifteen hundred and eighty-eight.

Boston Tea Party: 1783
   In seventeen hundred and seventy-three
   Bostonians filled their harbour with tea.

The relief of Mafeking: 1901
   The siege of Mafeking was undone
   In the year of nineteen hundred and one.

The Plague: 1665
   In sixteen hundred and sixty-five
   Thousands caught the plague and died.

The Charge of the Light Brigade: 1854
   They galloped to death in the Crimean War
   In eighteen hundred and fifty-four.

Another method you can use to remember some dates is to find something unusual about it. This will not work in every case but it is amazing what coincidences you will be able to find once you start looking for them:

For example The Second World War started on 3rd September, 1939. If you write this down in figures it becomes 3.9.39 which makes it look rather unusual. All you have to do is to remember the year and you will know the day and the month, and vice versa.

Here are a few more examples to give you some idea of the sort of thing you should be looking out for:

The only two British kings to abdicate, James II and Edward VIII, did so on the same day—12th December (James II in 1688 and Edward VIII in 1936).

There are some remarkable similarities between the lives of the two American Presidents, Abraham Lincoln and John Fitzgerald Kennedy, both of whom were assassinated (Lincoln in 1865, Kennedy in 1963). Lincoln was elected in 1860, Kennedy was elected one hundred years later in 1960. Both men were succeeded by a president named Johnson but the similarities do not end there for Andrew Johnson was born in 1808 and Lyndon Johnson was born in 1908!

It is not always possible, of course, to discover such neat links as that, but sometimes you will find you can make the link yourself with a bit of imagination. For example, Yuri Gagarin became the first man in space in 1961. Whilst in space he experienced weightlessness. This meant that if he had not been strapped into his seat he could have floated upside down. What has this got to do with the year 1961? Well, if you look at it again you will see that when you turn it upside down it remains the same!

43

Three Days' School a Year

Did you know that you go to school for only three whole days each year? Just follow the workings on this page and you will see that it appears to be true.

You sleep 8 hours a day.
8 × 365 = 2,920 hours   = 122 days per year

You have three meals a day, each of which lasts about an hour.
3 × 365 = 1,095 hours   = 46 days per year

You watch television for at least an hour each day, = 365 hours   = 15 days per year

There are 52 weekends in the year.   = 104 days per year

On an average, school holidays are 75 weekdays each year.   = 75 days per year

                                  362 days per year

As there are 365 days in a year there are only three days left for school, Hooray!

Whizzkid's Alphabet

This is a very old piece of fun.

A for horses	N for eggs
B for a rafter	O for my dead body
C for miles	P for a penny
D for dumb	Q for a bus
E for brick	R for mo
F for vescence	S for you
G for police	T for two
H for a scratch	U for mism
I for one	V for la France
J for oranges	W for a bet
K for teria	X for breakfast
L for leather	Y for girlfriend
M for sis	Z for a laugh

E for brick

R for MO

Fractured French

You will not find these in your French/English dictionary

French	English translation
Mal de mer	mail the horse
Coup de grace	cut the grass
Amoureuse	her hammer
Poussiniere	the cat's in there
Fil a plomb	feel a plum
Pas du tout	father of twins
Defense d'afficher	defend the fishes
Chien mechant	chain merchant
Ouvrez la fenetre	hoover the furniture
Entrez	on the tray
Je ne comprends pas	I do not understand father
Hore de combat	horse of war
Moi aussi	I am an Australian

Be a Mathematical Genius

The simplest way to become top in arithmetic is to develop an interest in numbers. This may sound more difficult than it really is. You will find, however, that once you begin to be interested in numbers, and what you can do with them, the better will be your results in arithmetic exams and tests.

One way to become interested in numbers is to learn some of the short cuts to calculation. Some of these short cuts will also help to provide an immediate improvement in your work and you will find that maths is probably not so difficult as you once imagined. Here are a few short cuts you may like to try. There is no need for you to learn them all. Try one or two and it will not be long before you will want to try some of the others.

TO MULTIPLY BY 25

It sounds impossible to multiply any number by 25 in your head but you can do it quite easily using this method.

All you have to do is add two noughts to the figure and then divide by 4. It is as simple as that!

Here is an example:

32×25
add two noughts $= 3,200$
divide by $4 = 800$

Therefore $32 \times 25 = 800$. Easy, isn't it!

Now try it with some other numbers. What is 17×25, 41×25, and 93×25? (If you get the answers 425, 1,025, and 2,325 you have got the idea.)

Really, to multiply by 5 is not very difficult but with long numbers you may find this method quicker.

All you have to do is divide by 2.

If the answer is exact, add a nought. If the answer has a remainder, add a 5.

That may sound strange, but here is an example:

$2,484 \times 5$
$2,484 \div 2 = 1,242$
Add a nought $= 12,420$

Therefore $2,484 \times 5 = 12,420$.

To multiply by 5

Here is another one:

$9,653 \times 5$
$9,653 \div 2 = 4,826$ with a remainder of 1.

As there is a remainder, you now add 5 to your main answer: 48,265

Therefore $9,653 \times 5 = 48,265$.

Do you want some more to try? Try multiplying each of these numbers by 5. 89,547, 3,201, 5,478, 7,326. (You should get the answers 447,735, 16,005, 27,390, 36,630).

TO DIVIDE BY 5

Again, you should find little difficulty in dividing by 5 but on some long numbers you may find it quicker to multiply by 2. Yes, that's right! When you have to divide a long number by 5, simply multiply it by 2.

Thus: $2,569,305 \div 5$
$2,569,305 \times 2 = 5,138,610$

Now all you have to do is knock off the last number and you have your answer for $2,569,305 \div 5 = 513,861$.

Here are some more you can try. Divide each of these numbers by 5: 98,305,675, 7,583,920, 34,975, 268,350. (You should get the answers 19,661,135, 1,516,784, 6,995, and 53,670.)

To divide
by 5

TO MULTIPLY BY 10

Surely you know this one! All you have to do is add a nought. So 53 times 10 is 530, 89 times 10 is 890 and 690,357,829 times 10 is 6,903,578,290. You're a mathematical genius!

You can use the same principle to multiply any number by 100, 1,000, or even 100,000. All you do is add the appropriate number of noughts.

Thus,
87×10	$= 870$
87×100	$= 8,700$
$87 \times 1,000$	$= 87,000$
$87 \times 100,000$	$= 8,700,000$

You can use the same method to multiply by any number ending in a nought. If, for example, you want to multiply a number by 300, first multiply by 3 and then add two noughts. So to multiply 12×300 you first say $12 \times 3 = 36$ and then add two noughts so that $12 \times 300 = 3,600$. In the same way, to multiply, for example, $15 \times 200,000$, all you do is say $15 \times 2 = 30$ and add five noughts so $15 \times 200,000 = 3,000,000$.

HOW TO CHECK AN ADDITION SUM

If you have to do an addition sum involving long numbers, here is a way to check whether or not you are likely to have the correct answer. Let us take the sum:

$$
\begin{array}{r}
26,936 \\
+\ 45,983 \\
\hline
72,919
\end{array}
$$

If you wish to make sure that you have the correct answer and you do not have time to do the sum again, or you do not want to do it again because it is so boring, you can check it this way: add together the individual numbers that make up the top number, 26936. $2+6+9+3+6 = 26$. Now add these numbers together. $2+6 = 8$. Remember the 8.

Do the same with the next number of the sum, and with the total reducing each one to a single digit number as we have just done.

This is what you will get:

$$
\begin{array}{rll}
26,936 = 26 & & = 8 \\
45,983 = 29 & = 11 & = 2 \\
\hline
72,919 = 28 & = 10 & = 1
\end{array}
$$

Adding together the numbers you have just arrived at, you get $8+2 = 10$. Reducing that down to one figure you say $1+0 = 1$, which is the figure you arrived at for the answer to your original sum.

This method is not absolutely foolproof, but it gives a pretty good indication of whether you are right or wrong. Suppose you had given the answer as 72,929. Adding these numbers together, 7+2+9+2+9, gives you 29. 2+9 = 11, and 1+1 = 2. When you add up the numbers at the side of the figure, 8+2 = 10 and 1+0 = 1, it does not equal the figure you have just arrived at for the total so you know that the total is wrong and you will have to check your addition again.

Although the method sounds a little complicated it is really quite simple and will provide you with a handy check on your additions.

A single digit

Two digits

take 1,000 lines..

Handy Magnifier

If a magnifying glass is needed to study something and there is no such thing readily available, the Whizzkid can come to the rescue with this handy magnifier. All you need to make it is a sheet of tin or some cooking foil. Make a hole through the tin with a nail. You need a perfectly round hole so place the tin on a piece of wood and then knock the nail through. Now place a drop of water on the hole. The easiest way to do this is to use a straw, or allow a drip to drop from the corner of a handkerchief that has been dipped in water.

Drop of Water

Strong Light

Sheet of tin or cooking foil

School Dinner

The bubble of water can now be used as a lens. Hold something underneath it and look at it through your water lens. You will find that you can obtain quite an appreciable magnification.

Try the same thing with different-sized holes and see which gives the best results. Be careful that you do not make the hole too big or it will not support the water.

After a while the water lens will evaporate or you may accidentally burst it, but it is an easy matter to put another drop of water on the hole.

For improved results, try using a drop of glycerine instead of water for the lens. Ask your science teacher for some glycerine from the school laboratory. He should have some unless, of course, the whole school has read this book and everyone is making these miniature magnifiers.

This handy magnifier is a useful thing to know should you ever want to observe something more closely than normal. You will find, however, that you will need a strong light source, such as a bright summer's day, to get the best results.

How to Come Top in Art

If you cannot draw a straight line but the art teacher is a bit of all right and you want to impress him or her, here is a little device that will help you to do it. Even if you have trouble drawing the curtains, or drawing money from your piggy bank, you can still be top of the class in art.

All you need is two solid blocks of wood. What? You don't know where to get a solid block of wood? Why don't you use your head!

With a saw, make a cut down the centre of each block almost to the bottom. Into the saw cuts you have just made, insert a sheet of ordinary glass.

Any picture that you would like to duplicate is placed on the table on one side of the glass. A piece of clean paper is placed on the table on the other side of the glass. If you look through the glass at an angle you will see a reflection of the picture. It is now quite a simple matter to follow the lines of the reflection with your pencil on the blank paper to produce a replica of the original drawing.

When using this method, watch out for things like clock faces, as a reverse image is produced so that everything, including the clock, will be drawn back to front.

GLASS

PENCIL

PAPER

ORIGINAL DRAWING

BLOCKS OF WOOD.

How to Prove 1=2

Here is something with which you can try to bamboozle your maths teacher.

This is how you do it:

Let us first assume that x = y.
If this is the case x—y must equal 0.
And, by the same reasoning, 2x—2y = 0.
If both these sums come to 0, we can therefore say that 2x—2y = x—y.

Write down this equation as follows:

$$2(x—y) = (x—y)$$

Divide each side of the equation by x—y.

It goes into the left-hand side twice and the right-hand side exactly once.

You therefore end up with the equation 2 = 1.

Let us assume....

Note for mathematical wizards: The reason why the above proof, although of course incorrect, actually works, is due to the fact that you cannot divide any sum by nothing. As x—y = 0, you have attempted to divide by nothing at one stage of the equation, but this just cannot be done. If your maths teacher is a little slow on the uptake you will fool him quite easily with this one.

55

How to Prove 3+3=8

Having proved to your teacher that 1 equals 2, you can now baffle him with more mathematical wizardry by proving that $3+3 = 8$.

You will need two pieces of tracing paper. On each sheet draw a large figure 3. It is as well to do this in ink so it is clearer.

Show the two pieces of tracing paper. Turn one of them around and then hold the two sheets together—whereupon it is plain to all that $3+3 = 8$!

How to Prove 1=0

Here is another mathematical equation you can try on your teacher. This one apparently proves that $1 = 0$.

Let $x = 1$.
Multiply both sides of the equation by x and you get $x2 = x$.
Take away 1 from each side and it becomes:
$$x2 - 1 = x - 1$$
This can also be expressed as:
$$(x+1)(x-1) = x-1$$
Now divide each side by x—1 and the answer is:
$$x+1 = 1$$
From this you can see that $x = 0$.

But right at the beginning we said that $x = 1$. It has therefore been proved that $1 = 0$.

WHIZZ KID
→

57

Classroom Changes

These two pictures show a typical classroom scene of Schoolditz, the well-known school from which no pupil has ever escaped. There are ten differences between the two pictures. Can you say what they are?

The answer is on page 127. 58

Facts to Bamboozle Teachers

Some amazing but true facts you can include in an appropriate essay to show how clever you are.

Ants have five noses.

Almost 250 people in India were killed by hailstones in 1888.

Russia has more frontiers than any other country.

Sharks can detect one part of blood in 100 million parts of water.

Anne Boleyn had six fingers on one hand.

A ten gallon hat holds about $\frac{3}{4}$ of a gallon.

The Emperor Nero played the bagpipes.

A human eye is made up of over 120,000,000 separate cells.

Birmingham is on the moon (it's a crater).

The average brain is 80 per cent water.

Date Palms

If you have trouble remembering the number of days in each month, your teacher will probably suggest that you learn the old rhyme:

> *Thirty days hath September,*
> *April, June, and November.*
> *All the rest have thirty-one,*
> *Excepting February alone,*
> *which has twenty-eight days clear*
> *and twenty-nine in each leap year.*

The rhyme itself takes a bit of remembering, but Whizzkids have another, easier, way of finding out the number of days in each month—they use a calendar!

If a calendar is not available you may like to try the date palm variety. All you need is a pair of hands. Go and get yourself a pair and you can test the method straight away. You've already got a pair? My, you are quick—you certainly are a Whizzkid!

Hold your hands palm upwards and take a look at them. Aren't they filthy. It's about time you took notice of your mother and washed them more often as she is always telling you.

From left to right, mentally label the fingers (ignore the thumbs) and the spaces in between the fingers with the name of the months in their correct order.

If a month falls on a finger it is very painful—no, if a month falls on a finger it has 31 days. All the months in between the fingers have 30 days.

The only exception in this method is February, which, as you of course know (from the rhyme that you have not bothered to learn), has only 28 days (29 in a leap year).

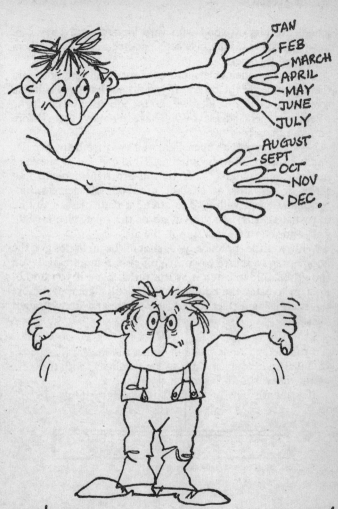

JAN
FEB
MARCH
APRIL
MAY
JUNE
JULY

AUGUST
SEPT
OCT
NOV
DEC.

DON'T FORGET TO IGNORE YOUR THUMBS!

Ruler Return

Rulers are bits of wood with very limited uses. They can, however, be made into an effective boomerang if two of them are joined together.

Get two wooden rulers and use four small screws to join them together at the centre. If you do not have any suitable screws a good strong glue will do the job just as well. If the rulers have metal edges, you will have to remove them before you join them together.

Now go out into an open area, well away from any people, and try out your new boomerang. Hold one end of one ruler in your right hand (assuming you are right-handed) and throw it upwards at a slant of about 80 degrees (unfortunately, you will have to attend a maths lesson to find out what that is). As you let go of the ruler, give a slight jerk, and the rulers will spin in the air.

With a little practice you should be able to get the boomerang to return to you. With even more practice, you should be able to catch it as it returns. Even if you do not manage to catch the boomerang, it is still a great deal more fun than using a ruler to measure things and draw straight lines.

Hidden Lessons

Hidden in this grid are the names of twelve lessons which teachers inflict upon innocent Whizzkids.

The lessons may be forwards, backwards, up and down, or diagonally. One has been ringed. See if you can find all the others.

```
A L G E C I T E M H T I R A
B F R E N C H E M I S T R Y
I S T R O I N R U S S T A R
O M P R S G I N S T R U A T
L A R T L O R A I M P E G E
O L O I B O A A C M U S U M
G R S L M H N C P R E H I O
Y H A L G E B R A H R I S E
B I L A M I S C I S Y H P G
```

For answer see p. 127.

Revising for Exams

As most Whizzkids know, the easy way to pass exams is, of course, . . . cheat. Unfortunately, this is a very risky method, and you are almost certain to be caught in the act—particularly as the examiner probably knows all the tricks of the cheating trade as that is how he got through his exams. It would seem, therefore, that there is no sure way to pass exams except by working at the subject. There are, however, several ways you can improve your chances.

The first thing to do is start your revising of the subject well before the exam is due. It is of little use trying to cram all you need to know into your head the night before the exam. You should start your revision at least two months beforehand.

Before you start any revision, try to discover your best time for studying. Some Whizzkids find it best to get up early and study before breakfast. They are at their brightest then and they have the added advantage that the house is quiet and this makes studying easier. Other people find that their minds are more active in the evening and so they do their studying then. Try studying at different times to find out when your brain is at its most receptive and then arrange your study timetable to fit in with this time.

Always make up a timetable for your revision. This is particularly important if you have several subjects to study. Allocate a set amount of time for each subject so you can be sure you will cover everything of importance by the day of the exam. Having set yourself a timetable, stick to it. It is tempting at times to watch a favourite television programme or go out with your friends instead of studying. If you give in to this temptation you will not be able to get through everything on time. There will be plenty of time for relaxation after the exams.

It is often a good idea to use more than your normal text book and notes for revision. Try to find another book on the subject you are studying. You may be so familiar with your usual books that you will not take too much notice of what is in them. New books will stimulate your mind, perhaps give you some fresh ideas on the subject, explain things that you did not understand fully before, and provide you with information and facts that you did not know of previously.

C

You may find it worthwhile to revise with a friend of the same ability as yourself. Your study periods will become more interesting as a result, for you can ask one another questions or generally discuss the subject. This is much better than trying to learn a subject parrot-fashion.

Most exam papers tend to follow similar patterns each year. Ask your teacher if you can take a look at previous exam papers so you can study them. This will give you a general indication of what questions are usually asked. Try answering the questions set in previous years. It is a good idea to give yourself only the time allowed in the exam to answer the question.

You may find it worthwhile to revise with a friend of the same ability as yourself...

Boosting Your Brainpower

To get the best results from any form of revision you need to have your brain working at its maximum power. There are several simple techniques you can adopt to help you achieve this.

First you should always try to work in a quiet atmosphere where you will not be interrupted. If you are lucky enough to have your own bedroom, shut yourself in it during your study periods and put a 'Do Not Disturb' notice on the door. Make sure that everyone knows the times you have reserved for study so they will not annoy you when you are trying to work.

try the
local
park

If it is not possible to shut yourself away, you could always try shutting the rest of the family away while you work! Another alternative is to do your studying in the local library. This is a particularly useful place because you have reference books to hand with which you can check facts and perhaps discover things that are not in your own books. If the library is too far from your home, why not have a word with your teacher to see if you can study in the classroom for a while after everyone else has gone home? If none of these places is available you can always do your studying in your garden or the local park—provided that it is not raining.

Studying outside is a useful thing to try because it provides you with the oxygen that your brain needs to function at full power. You should also bear this in mind when studying at home and make sure the room in which you are working is well ventilated, well illuminated, and neither too cold nor too hot. If it is too cold you will spend all your time rubbing your hands together and doing exercises to keep warm. If it is too hot you will probably fall asleep.

Although you do not wish to fall asleep during your study periods, sleep is another essential factor in keeping your brain working efficiently. You must have sufficient rest. If you stay up every night to watch the late film on television your brain will be weary and your study periods will be affected. Adequate sleep is essential if you wish to pass your exams with flying colours.

To help you study more effectively and get your brain working at full steam you should also take regular exercise. Don't catch the school bus—cycle to school. Get out for walks or play games every weekend—it's true that a healthy body and a healthy mind go together. You will be fitter, more alert, and better able to cope with your studies.

Tips for Exams

Here are a few other tips you can try to improve your chances:

Listen carefully to any instructions given by the invigilator·

Work out how long you should spend on each question. This will help you make sure that you do not waste time.

When working out this time, allow half an hour free. Fifteen minutes of this should be used at the beginning of the exam to read through the questions. The other fifteen minutes is to be used at the end of the ordeal to check your answers and make sure you have not done anything silly.

Do not attempt to answer any question until you have read it at least a couple of times.

Do not attempt to answer any question until you are certain you understand it.

Write neatly. If doing mathematical questions make sure the figures are clear and presented logically.

There is usually no need to answer the questions in the correct order provided that you number the answers clearly. So tackle the easiest question first. It will give you a good start and boost your morale ready for the harder questions.

If you have to write an essay and cannot seem to get it started satisfactorily leave a space at the head of the page and start writing the second paragraph. When you have finished the essay go back and write the beginning paragraph. You should now find that it is easier to write.

To make sure your essay is presented in a logical sequence, jot down on a sheet of paper the main points you wish to mention. This will also help to ensure that you do not miss out anything important.

If while writing you want to put down a name or a date and it will not come to mind at the crucial moment, don't worry. Leave a space for the information and carry on writing. You will probably find the missing fact will spring to mind later—probably when you are answering another question! You can then go back and fill in the space. If it does not spring to mind by the end of the exam just leave the space blank. Provided your answers are reasonable and presented neatly, the blank space is not likely to affect your result.

Although you have answered the easiest questions first and the hardest questions last, do not hand in the paper in that order. If you are allowed to present the paper in any order, put your best answers in the first and last positions. Put the poorest answers in the middle. Although this sequence will not guarantee a pass, it could help to persuade the examiner to give you a slightly better mark than he might otherwise have done because he will start and end his marking session with a good impression of your abilities.

N.B.
This sequence will not - - - - - -
GUARANTEE A PASS

How to Come First in Athletics

METHOD ONE: Come Last

The easiest way to be a winner in athletics is to only enter for the long-distance races. If the race is around an oval or circular track all you have to do is lag behind until the very last lap. Wait until the leading runner is almost up to you and then run as fast as you can until you reach the finishing line. With a bit of luck most of the spectators will think you have come in first and will cheer you like mad.

and cheer like mad...

METHOD TWO: The Short Cut

The same technique can be used in cross-country races. Here you must first study the course until you can find a practical short cut. During the race, make use of this short cut and then lie in wait until the first runner (or, if you are really subtle, the second or third runner) passes you. Making

sure that no-one sees you, you slip from your hiding place and rejoin the race completely fresh and able to make a spirited appearance along the final run.

METHOD THREE: The Hidden Bicycle Trick

Some cross-country races are also suitable for this great technique. A bike is hidden in some bushes near the start of the race. You run to where it is hidden and then cycle towards the end of the course. Once you have re-hidden the bike you can make your final run as the other competitors stagger towards the finish.

Shorter races are a little more difficult. In these your only hope of winning is to either cripple the best runners, or make sure that you get an extremely good start. There are at least five ways in which you can ensure that this will happen:

1. Tie rockets to your shoes
2. Tie weights to the shoes of your opponents
3. Tie your opponents' shoelaces together
4. Make sure that the starting blocks of the other runners are so soft that the spikes of their running shoes will stick into them. While they are trying to extricate their spikes you will be well away
5. Put cotton wool in the ears of your opponents so they will not hear the starting gun

Other athletic events present some difficulties. Most Whizzkids will try to avoid them if they can—after all you cannot be expected to be brilliant in everything. If, however, you are determined to enter for throwing events, you can put some glue on the discus, javelin, or cricket ball used by your opponents. That should cramp their style a little. To get good results in throwing events you need two accomplices. As you are about to throw, the first person shouts "Look!" and points to the sky. When everyone looks up, you quickly drop the thing you are about to throw. At the same time your second friend, who is at the far end of the field, drops a duplicate discus, javelin, or cricket ball on the ground. As all the spectators and the judges have been distracted at the crucial moment they will think you have made your throw and you should win the contest. (When using this technique make sure that your mate at the far end of the field knows exactly what you are throwing. It could jeopardise your chances if the javelin you have thrown turns into a cricket ball in mid-air . . .)

How to Write a Masterpiece

You need three things to write a masterpiece: pen or pencil, paper, and a brain. The writing implement and the paper are fairly easy to obtain. A brain is a little more difficult. You could, of course, always ask for a transplant. There are two problems with this solution—the transplanted brain might reject your body, and suitable brains are not easy to come by, for the majority of people with brains are not prepared to part with them. This being the case, we must see if there is some other way of writing a masterpiece.

And there is!

Here, for the benefit of all Whizzkids is the easy way to write a Masterpiece.

The method can be explained quite simply—use big words.

Big words impress teachers, especially if they do not know what they mean. Take a look through a dictionary and make a note of the biggest and most complicated words you can find. Drop a few of them into your next essay. It probably won't make sense, but your teacher may not notice this.

Another way to write a masterpiece is to carry a Masterpiece Creator around with you. This is simply a paragraph that makes very little sense with several alternative words inserted at intervals. Here is an example. Copy it on to a postcard and you will be ready to write a masterpiece at a moment's notice.

	circumjacence		leit-motiv
	encompassment		field of enquiry
The	environment	to which this	supposition
	entourage		

	intrinsic		sacrosanct			correlation
is	vivicatery	is	honorific	to the		amplitude
	prometheatery		ostentatious			magnitude
	symbiotic		aureoleous			relative quantity

	qualified		field of enquiry	Professionals
	pertinent		leit-motiv	Savants
that is	apposite	to this	proposition	Scholars
	relevant		supposition	

	moralised		denouement	
	deliberated		repercussions	
have	hortated	over the	contingencies	of this
	sat in conclave		precipitations	

milieu	ineffectively	Strategists	
circumstance	unproductively	Experts	
situation	ingloriously	Virtuosos	but
environment	negatively	Practitioners	

interlocute	consequence	supporters	
pontificate	derivative	coadjutors	
intercommunicate	the denouement	of this but advocates	
dialogise			

	unempowered	evaluate	advantages
	unauthorised	to appraise the	effectiveness of such
are	unqualified	estimate	efficacy
		assess	

endeavour
action
measures

To use the Masterpiece Creator, all you have to do is write this paragraph out two or three times using a different combination of alternative words on each occasion and you will have a masterpiece to be proud of. If you wish to write a longer masterpiece change some of the other words as well. Your finished essay will probably not make sense but who is to know? In any case, geniuses seldom do make sense so you will be in good company.

To show you how effective the Masterpiece Creator is, here is a short example:

The circumjacence which this leit-motiv be intrinsic is sacrosanct to the correlation that is qualified to this field of enquiry. Professionals have moralised over the denouement of this milieu but ineffectively. Strategists interlocute the consequence of this but supporters are unempowered to evaluate the advantages of such endeavour. The encompassment which this supposition be vivicatery is honorific to the amplitude that is deliberated over the leit-motiv. Savants have deliberated over the repercussions of this circumstance but unproductively. Experts potificate the derivative of this but coadjutors are unauthorised to appraise the effectiveness of such action.

Sounds good, doesn't it? Let's hope it isn't rude!

Pen Stand

One of the problems when doing homework is that of keeping pens, pencils, and, most necessary of all, rubbers in place. If you make this simple pen stand your problems will be solved. In fact, you will find it so handy you will probably decide to make two—one for home and one to go on your desk at school.

All you need is a sheet of fairly heavy card cut into the shape shown. Cut along the dotted lines and then bend the card into shape. Glue the edges of the base tray into position, pull out the pen holder tabs, and then fold back the bracket and slip one end of it through the back of the holder to hold the whole stand in place. If needed the bracket can be easily undone and the whole stand folded up for carrying from one classroom to another.

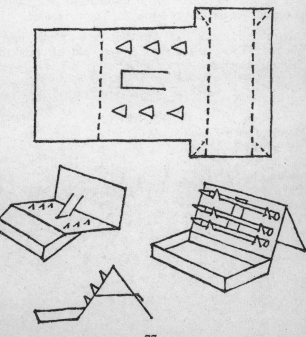

How Old is Your Teacher?

Most teachers look pretty ancient, but you can discover the exact age of your teacher with the following ruse:

Ask the teacher to think of the number of the month in which she (or he) was born. January counts as 1, February as 2, March as 3 and so on.

She is then to double that number.

Then add 5 to the total.

And multiply the answer by 50.

Now ask her to add her age to the sum.

And then subtract 250 from the total.

If she now tells you the answer you will know in which month she was born and how ancient she is. If the answer is composed of three digits, the first is the number of the month and the last two are her age. When there are four numbers in the answer the first two will give you the month.

Here are two examples: Mrs. Bounce the games mistress was born in August and she is 93 years old. Mr. Stinks the chemistry teacher was born in December and he is 78 years old.

	Bounce	*Stinks*
Month of birth	(Aug) 8	(Dec) 12
Multiply by 2	16	24
Add 5	21	29
Multiply by 50	1,050	1,450
Add age	(93) 1,143	(78) 1,528
Subtract 250	893	1,278

Make a Teacher-Distracter

Cut out a large triangle (A) from a sheet of card. The sort of card used for cereal packets is ideal. From a sheet of brown paper cut out a smaller triangle (B). The base of the small triangle is the same as the base of the large one but it is only half the height.

Glue the base of the small triangle to the base of the large triangle. When the glue has dried, fold the two together as shown.

If you hold the card at point C and flick your hand down sharply, the paper triangle will fold outwards with a loud snap. Do it in class and your teacher will wonder what has happened. The only snag is that you, or possibly the whole class, may receive detention or some other equally horrible punishment for perpetrating this bit of harmless fun. You have been warned!

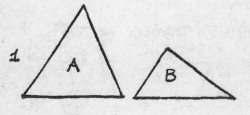

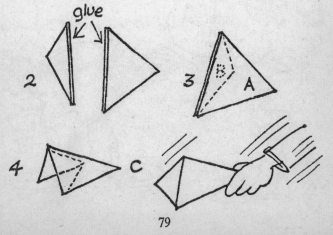

Computer Cards

If you would like your teachers to think you are brilliant at arithmetic, make up a set of the cards shown opposite. Cut square holes in each of the cards where shown. You now have a set of magic computer cards that will tell you any number thought of by a teacher or a friend.

Hand the six number cards to your teacher and ask him to think of any number from 1 to 63. You keep the blank card. While the teacher is thinking of a number, ask him to return to you all the cards that bear his selected number.

Place these cards together in any order and put the blank card on top of the pile. Add together the numbers visible through the holes in the blank card. The total you get, assuming that you have added correctly, will be the number thought of by your teacher.

If he asks you how it is done just tell him that you are a natural mathematical genius.

While the teacher is thinking of a number....

I'm a natural born genius

45	63	27	10	58	9	61	42
29	8	11	57	30	59	☐	62
13	24	☐	60	40	47	14	56
46	☐	12	44	☐	25	☐	27
43	15	41	31	26	62	12	28

33	49	27	17	21	55	61	39
3	☐	31	51	63	43	☐	13
15	7	1	19	15	23	59	41
57	☐	29	9	☐	35	☐	51
53	5	47	25	45	33	11	37

54	23	18	58	63	31	26	51
29	☐	61	50	20	27	☐	52
56	28	☐	17	59	48	21	60
31	☐	19	55	☐	30	16	53
62	49	24	57	22	52	27	25

11	38	62	51	43	26	55	15
10	☐	63	35	31	19	☐	46
14	3	☐	59	27	7	58	18
25	☐	6	47	2	39	☐	22
54	23	50	30	35	42	11	34

5	47	28	53	61	13	20	52
37	☐	44	30	46	55	4	7
22	63	☐	12	62	14	60	31
23	☐	29	54	☐	15	☐	6
45	36	39	21	47	28	63	38

39	63	54	38	45	61	49	33
53	☐	57	46	43	41	☐	62
34	40	☐	55	42	51	59	35
60	32	44	59	☐	58	☐	58
36	48	50	56	52	47	42	37

More Facts to Bamboozle Teachers

George Washington once had a set of false teeth made of iron—until they went rusty!

In London it rains more on Thursday than on any other day of the week.

King Louis XIV of France never washed.

Queen Anne was buried in a square coffin.

There are 66 books, 1,189 chapters, and 31,173 verses in the Bible.

A bucket of hot water will freeze faster than a bucket of cold water.

The longest-named muscle in the human body is the *levator labii aleoquae nasi*. It is in the upper lip.

Admiral Lord Nelson suffered from acute sea sickness.

A man's brain is larger than a woman's.

London's underground railway system is the oldest and the biggest in the world.

Cleopatra, Queen of Egypt, was Greek.

The smallest spider in the world is found in Samoa. It is the Patu Marplesi and is .43mm in length.

Music in Science

Next time you are sitting in the science laboratory waiting for a lesson, make the time pass more agreeably with some music. All you need is a plastic drinking straw, a length of rubber tubing from the laboratory, and a funnel which you should also find in the laboratory.

Cut a long V shape in either side of one end of the straw. Put the straw into your mouth and hold it between your teeth just beyond the end of the V. Now blow and you should get a soft buzzing sound. To make the sound more effective, tape the rubber tubing to the end of the straw and then stick the funnel into the other end.

grip with teeth...

zzzzzz

How to Be a Lightning Calculator

If there is a thunderstorm while you are at school you can amaze the class by telling them how far away the storm is. All you have to do is to measure the time in seconds between the flash of lightning and the next clap of thunder and then divide by 5. As sound travels at about a fifth of a mile per second the answer to this calculation will tell you how many miles the storm is away from you.

By doing the same calculation for subsequent flashes of lightning you will be able to deduce whether the storm is moving closer or further away from you.

(If someone asks you how you do it, just say, "It was just a flash of inspiration.")

How to Produce Thunder

After amazing the class with your lightning calculation you can then go on to tell them that you can produce thunder of your own. All you need is a long piece of string. Cut a short piece off the string and then tie the long length to the centre of the short length.

Ask a friend to hold the ends of the short piece in his ears while you draw your finger and thumb along the long piece. Much to his surprise he will be able to hear a noise that sounds amazingly like that of thunder.

Simple Multiplication

Here is a simple way to multiply any two-figure number by another two-figure number. All you have to be able to do is multiply by 2, divide by 2, and add up a column of figures.

As an example we will try multiplying 26×54.

First you have to write the numbers down, side by side.

Now divide the figure on the left by 2 and multiply the number on the right by 2. Continue doing this until the number on the left is reduced to 1. With the example given (26×54) your piece of paper should look like this:

26	54
13	108
$6\frac{1}{2}$	216
3	432
$1\frac{1}{2}$	864

In doing this you should ignore any remainders that appear on numbers in the left-hand column. The next step is to draw a line through any number in the right-hand column that has to its left an even number. If you do this with the example it will look like this:

26	54
13	108
6	216
3	432
1	864

If you now add together all the numbers that remain in the right-hand column the total will be the answer to the multiplication. Thus, in this example, $108 + 432 + 864 = 1,404$ and, yes you've guessed it, $26 \times 54 = 1,404$.

Here is another example: 44×72

44	72
22	144
11	288
5	576
2	1,152
1	2,304

$288 + 576 + 2,304 = 3,168$ so $44 \times 72 = 3,168$.   Simple, isn't it!

Create Concrete Conkers

The ultimate aim of all conker players is to own a conker that is so hard it will defeat all its opponents. When such a conker makes its appearance it is usually owned by a Whizzkid. This is because many Whizzkids harden their conkers by various means—some fair and some foul.

There are several recipes that are claimed to produce a really hard conker. One is to soak the conker in vinegar for a day or two and then let it dry out. Another method states that the best thing to do is to bake the conker for about a quarter of an hour in a very low oven. Some Whizzkids prefer to combine these two techniques by soaking the conkers in vinegar before cooking them.

Whizzkids who have a coal fire in their house will find that if they put the conker up the chimney for a day or so while the fire is in use it will produce a nice hard conker.

Another way, if you have the patience, is to leave the conker on your windowsill for a year, by which time it should be really hard—or it may have gone mouldy! The more usual reason for the failure of this method is that mothers, who do not understand what the important things in life are, object to conkers on windowsills and throw them away.

For the really determined Whizzkid, the only sure-fire way to harden a conker is to cut it in half and remove the flesh from inside the skin. The hollow shell is then filled with concrete and when this has set the two halves are glued back together. Unfortunately, some purists regard this as cheating!

Flour Power

All Whizzkids should know a few practical jokes. This one will take a little while to make, but it is well worth the effort. It is particularly useful if you have a teacher who smokes. (Most of them steam a lot but only a few actually smoke.)

Glue a piece of card into a matchbox as shown in the first illustration. On top of this you must fix a small triangle of card that will just fit into the box when the drawer is closed. Having done this, open the drawer once again and drill a hole through the end of the flap and a hole through the end of the drawer. Tie a piece of elastic through these two holes and draw it tight so it tends to pull the flap upwards. The Whizzkid's matchbox booby trap is now ready for action.

Place a small container of flour, a dead fly, a worm, or, if you have no imagination—a button, on the flap. Push the flap down and then close the box. Leave the matchbox where your victim is likely to spot it.

The triangle on the flap will hold the flap down while the box is closed but as soon as it is opened the flap is released and the contents will leap out.

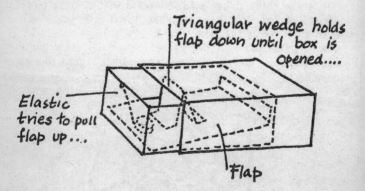

Triangular wedge holds flap down until box is opened....

Elastic tries to pull flap up...

Flap

How to Be Instantly Ill (in Moments of Crisis)

1. Paleface Technique. Put talcum powder on your face to make yourself look pale. Do not overdo this or a cloud of powder will permeate the room when you sneeze, bend down to do up your shoelaces, or scratch your nose.

This technique was originally conceived by an Indian boy—he became the first paleface. It was he that coined the well-known phrase "A bit of talcum is always walcum."

2. The Plague. For a really spectacular effect put some spots on your face, hands, and body. There are several ways you can do this. Cut some spot-shaped pieces from red sticky paper. If your dog is called 'Spot' do not cut out the pieces to his shape or the ruse will not work. Stick the bits of paper on yourself. Do not use this method for spots on the body as they have a tendency to drop off. The inside of your clothes will end up spottier than the outside of your skin.

A more reliable method is to use lipstick (make sure you use lipstick of an appropriate colour). If lipstick is not

readily available you could use red ink but it is harder to remove when you wish to make a rapid recovery.

3. Instant Mumps. Put cotton wool between your lower teeth and your cheeks. Mind you do not swallow the cotton wool—or talk.

4. Headache. A subtle technique. Apart from acting ability, nothing is needed to fake a headache as no-one else can prove whether you are really suffering or not. Half close your eyes. Do not comb your hair. Hold your hand to your forehead when your mother is *not* looking. As soon as she spots you, count silently to three and then take your hand away. In the hands of a professional Whizzkid this last trick can be extremely effective.

5. Highly Dangerous Method. This technique can backfire in the hands of a novice and should only be used as a last resort—very carefully. It should be combined with one or more of the other methods already described. The trick is to say that you *want* to go to school even though you are obviously not well enough to do so. If you overdo it your mother may believe you.

Calendar for History

This calendar will come in handy during history lessons. You can use it to calculate the specific day of the week on which a particular historical event occurred. The calendar works with any date from 1752 up to the year 2099 so you can use it for future dates as well. Write the whole thing on a postcard (use both sides of the card if necessary) and you will always have it to hand when you need it.

To find the day on which an event occurred, this is what you do:

Take the last two figures of the year.

Divide by 4 (ignore any remainders) and add this to the two figures.

Add the day of the month.

Add the number for the century according to the 'Century Table'.

Add the number for the month as given in the 'Month Table'.

Divide by 7.

Look up the remainder obtained from this last sum on the 'Day Table' and you will then know on which day your particular event occurred.

Here is an example to show you how easy it is to do:
The first successful ascent of Mount Everest was achieved on 29th May, 1953. What day of the week was it?

The last two figures of the year are 5 and 3	53
Dividing by 4 gives 14 (ignore the remainder)	13
Add the day of the month (29th)	29
Add the century number (20th century = 0)	0
Add the month number (May = 2)	2
	97

Now divide the total by 7. 7 goes into 97 over 13 times. Take the remainder, which in this case is six, and look it up on the day table (6= Friday). You now know that Everest was conquered on Friday, 29th May, 1953.

CENTURY TABLE

Century	add
18th	4
19th	2
20th	0
21st	6

MONTH TABLE

Month	add	
Jan.	1	(If a Leap Year add 0)
Feb.	4	(If a Leap Year add 3)
March	4	
April	0	
May	2	
June	5	
July	0	
Aug.	3	
Sept.	6	
Oct.	1	
Nov.	4	
Dec.	6	

DAY TABLE

Value	Day
0	Saturday
1	Sunday
2	Monday
3	Tuesday
4	Wednesday
5	Thursday
6	Friday

You will notice that January and February each have two month values. The lower of the two values is used only if the year in question is a Leap Year.

If the last two figures of the year divide by 4 exactly then it is a Leap Year. Thus 1916, 1732 and 1968 were all Leap Years. If the year in question is the last one of a particular century it is a Leap only if the complete year is divisible by 400. The only year this affects on this calendar is the year 2000 which will be a Leap Year. The other two century years covered, 1800 and 1900, are not exactly divisible by 400 so they were not Leap Years.

IF the last two figures of the year divide by 4 exactly then it is a "LEAP" YEAR!

1916

1732

1968

Who Teaches What?

The pictures show several schoolteachers. From the clues given, can you name each of the teachers shown? You are allowed to consult a dictionary to look at any words you do not know.

Mr 'Nosey' Parker who teaches Latin has a Roman nose (*some people say it's roamin' all over his face*).

Sports master 'Jogging' Jim Nasium is tonsured.

Headmaster Ivor Grudge is hirsuite.

English master Sammy Colon is obese.

Brad Awl the woodwork master is myopic.

'Spud' Murphy the gardening instructor has a cauliflower ear.

Mark Time the music teacher is cadaverous.

Answers on page 127.

Picture the Map

A useful way to remember the basic outline of a country when drawing maps is to picture part or all of the country as a familiar shape. The most obvious example of this is Italy which looks like a boot. Most people know this and can draw a reasonable map of Italy. You can, however, take this a stage further by visualising the island of Sicily as a ball that the boot is about to kick. If you stretch your imagination a little more you may be able to see Sardinia and the northern coast of Tunisia as forming the goalposts through which Italy hopes to kick the ball.

ITALY

IT'S A GOAL !

TUNISIA

On the other side of the world you will find a similar example with New Zealand which also forms the shape of a boot. (Perhaps it is a wellington boot as Wellington is the capital of New Zealand.) In this case the ball (Australia) is so large that the boot has broken in two and turned upside down in the process of kicking it.

THE BROKEN LEG OF NEW ZEALAND

See if you can see any other shapes on the map of the world. Take a look at South America. It looks a little like the head of an elephant. Once you can see the shape, compare it to India and Africa (both the home of the elephant) which both have the same basic shape.

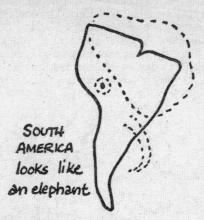

SOUTH
AMERICA
looks like
an elephant

Some other things you can look out for are the shoe that forms Israel, turn Mongolia upside down and it looks like a rhinoceros, if you turn Austria over it looks rather like a buzzard. And whilst thinking about birds take a look at New Guinea where you will see a bird in flight (perhaps it is a Guinea fowl). Look at Crete and you will see the same bird but now it must be asleep for it is lying on its back! Use your imagination to see what other shapes you can

NEW GUINEA
is like a bird
in flight

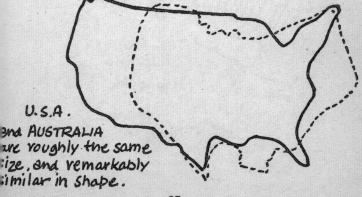

MONGOLIA
(upside down)
looks like a Rhino

find around the world. It will help you to remember what the various countries look like.

As you look you may notice other things that will help you come top in geography. The coast of Europe and North Africa fits almost exactly into the coastline of the United States and South America. If you can draw one of these coastlines you have only to reverse the picture in your mind and you are well on the way to drawing the other. And if you can draw the United States you can draw Australia for they are both about the same size and remarkably alike in shape, especially if you turn one of them upside down.

U.S.A.
and AUSTRALIA
are roughly the same
size, and remarkably
similar in shape.

D

To draw any map from memory is quite simple if you are prepared to spend a little time developing the skill.

First take a good look in your atlas at the country you wish to draw. Now close the book and draw the map from memory. If you can form any of the mental pictures just mentioned you will find it a great help for this initial stage. When you have finished drawing, compare your effort with the map in the atlas. Do not worry if it is not too accurate on this first attempt. The principal aim of your first drawing is to just get a general idea of the shape and proportion of the country.

When you have seen where you went wrong on your first attempt, close the atlas and have another go. Keep repeating this procedure — drawing — comparison — drawing — comparison—and you will find your efforts improving quite rapidly. It will not be too long before you can draw an accurate representation every time.

The same technique can be used for the placing of rivers, cities, mountains, and similar items on your maps. Doing it this way will help to implant the information in your brain and you will soon be well on the way to being top of the class in geography.

THE AUSTRIAN
BUZZARD
(Map upside down)

ISRAEL

In the Picture

Every year the pupils and staff of Schoolditz Concentration Camp (We have ways of making you concentrate) line up for a school photograph. The two photographs shown here look exactly the same at first sight but there are, in fact, ten subtle differences. Can you see them?

The answer is on page 127.

Hexagon Magic

Here is a little novelty you can make to amuse your maths teacher. Trace the nest of hexagons shown here on to a sheet of paper and write in the numbers 1 to 49 as shown.

The amazing thing about this formation is that any group of seven hexagons will add up to 175. Furthermore, if you add up the numbers in each row of seven hexagons you will find that—yes, that's right—they add up to 175. But they are not the only amazing thing about this magic hexagon figure, for there are, in addition, over two hundred combinations of non-adjacent hexagons that will add up to the same total as well. The easiest way to show some of these combinations is to cut out bits of paper to the shapes shown. In each of these cases the numbers visible when you place the paper directly over the hexagon grid will add up to 175.

When you have shown these to your maths teacher and the rest of your class, get them all trying to discover some of the remaining two hundred hexagon combinations that add up to the magic number 175.

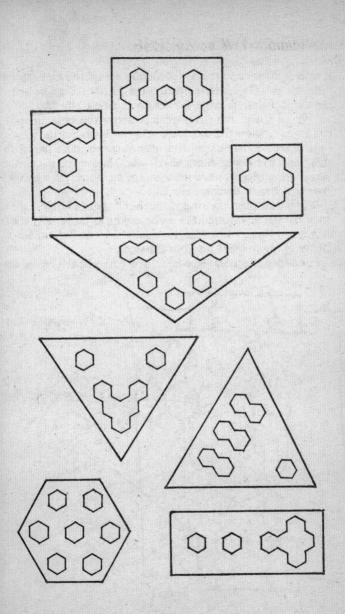

Make Your Teacher Roll Her Eyes

It is easy to make your teacher roll her eyes if you make this little gadget. On an envelope draw a picture of a teacher. Do the drawing as large as possible for best effect.

Make a slit in the envelope just above the head of the picture and below the shoulders. Cut out holes for the eyes.

Now take a strip of paper a little narrower than the two slits you have made in the envelope. Measure the distance between the two eyes and draw on the strip two thick wavy lines at the same distance apart.

If you now push the strip through the slits and pull it the lines are visible through the eyeholes and it looks as if the eyes are rolling from side to side which should provide plenty of amusement for your classmates.

For added effect draw the lines in several different colours.

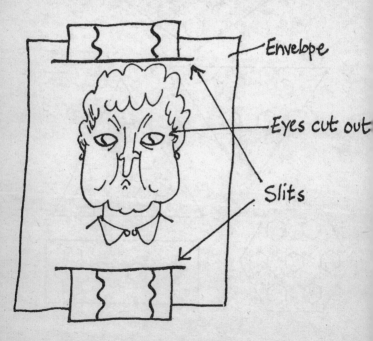

Envelope

Eyes cut out

Slits

Make Your Teacher Vanish!

Make your teacher vanish—it sounds like a dream come true!

Draw a picture of your teacher and a stick of chalk as shown on this page. Now hold the drawing about 50 centimetres from your face and close your left eye. Concentrate your gaze on the stick of chalk and slowly move the drawing nearer to your face. Keep looking at the chalk and suddenly your teacher will disappear.

If you continue moving the drawing towards you your teacher will appear once again.

0

Letters of Memory

A useful trick to remember when you want to memorise a list of related items is to take their initial letters and form them into a word or a sentence. In the majority of cases you will find it a lot easier to remember the single word or the sentence than the list of items. Take, for example, the Great Lakes of America: Huron, Ontario, Michigan, Erie, Superior. Their initial letters form the word HOMES. If you prefer to form the initial letters into a sentence, how about Some Men Hate Eating Oranges; the initial letter of each word standing for the initial letter of each lake, from west to east.

It is best if you make up these words and sentences for yourself, as you will then find them even easier to remember, but here are a few more examples to get you going:

In music, the lines of the treble, the letters of which are E.G.B.D.F., can be remembered by the phrase Every Good Boy Deserves Favours.

The spaces of the treble clef are F.A.C. and E, which make the single word FACE.

To remember the colours of the spectrum, form them into the name of an imaginary scientist ROY G. BIV and you will know the colours are Red, Orange, Yellow, Green, Blue, Indigo, and Violet.

Would you like to remember the names of the planets of the Solar System in order from the Sun? Then see if the sentence Space Men Vote Earth Most Jolly of the Solar Universe's Nine Planets will help you to recall Sun, Mercury, Venus, Earth, Mars, Jupiter, Saturn, Uranus, Neptune, and Pluto.

Teacher! Teacher!

Teacher! Teacher! Can you help me out?
Certainly, which way did you come in?

Teacher! Teacher! My knees keep knocking.
Well, tie some cymbals to them and join the school band.

Teacher! Teacher! Why do you call me Pilgrim?
Because you're making a little progress.

Teacher! Teacher! Why do you think I'm a monster?
Be quiet and comb your face.

Teacher! Teacher! Why do you keep me in this cage?
Because you're the teacher's pet.

Teacher! Teacher! Why is the wife of a Sultan called a Sultana?
It stands to raisin.

Teacher! Teacher! Why do you think I'm a Hindu?
Because you're always off Sikh.

Make a Teacher-Scarer

Well, I don't advise you to scare a teacher with one of these nifty little devices, but hide one or more of them inside your next-door-pupil's book and watch him jump out of his skin when the book is opened!

All you need is two pieces of paper each measuring about 10×10 centimetres and an elastic band.

Roll each sheet of paper into a tight roll. Do this as tightly as you can but do not worry too much if it unrolls slightly when you release your hold on it.

Now twist the elastic band several times around the centre of the two rolls of paper to join them together. Bend each roll in half at the centre and twist them in opposite directions until the elastic band is as tight as you can manage.

Now all you have to do is place the device in a book or under something on a desk and wait. When the object is picked up the the Teacher Scarer will leap into the air with a loud whirring.

Elastic Band.

Twist round

Which School ?

1. What school did Jane attend in Charlotte Brontë's novel *Jane Eyre*?

2. Which fictional school for girls was created by the cartoonist Ronald Searle?

3. Billy Bunter is the famous pupil of which fictitious school?

4. This school is famous for its Wall Game.

5. Which school was attended by Nigel Molesworth in the books by Geoffrey Willans and Ronald Searle?

6. In the novel *Tom Brown's Schooldays*, what is the famous school attended by Tom?

7. HRH Prince Charles received part of his education at a school in Scotland. Can you name it?

8. What was the name of the school at which the cruel Mr. Squeers taught in *Nicholas Nickleby*?

9. Can you name the school attended by Sir Winston Churchill?

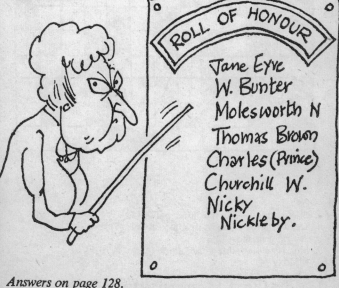

Answers on page 128.

Whizzkid's Crossword

Across

1. Silent acting—it comes after panto (4)
4. Dead language taught in some schools (5)
8. All right in short (2)
9. Sing (or do anything else) alone (4)
10. Midday (4)
11. Tidy (4)
13. At school it could be language or literature (7)
16. A gigantic person of superhuman strength (5)
18. Fee—Fo Fum, I smell the blood of an Englishman (2)

20. It describes a noun (9)
22. Of the same class or family (3)
23. French for 'some' (2)
25. Old you (2)
27. Rung between lessons (4)
29. I am this—and so are you (2)
30. A perfume of roses, some call it 'attar' (4)
31. Short Order of the British Empire (3)
33. Opposite of don't (2)
34. James, he invented the steam engine (4)
37. Public house—not out? (3)
39. Painting is done in this lesson (3)
42. Accident cases are often carried on this (9)
44. To perform (3)
45. They go with pans (4)
47. Initially limited (3)
48. Shoulder blade (7)
49. Unknown writer (4)

Down

1. Tedious sameness (8)
2. Nickname used for American President Eisenhower (3)
3. French is (3)
4. Henry Wadsworth—, author of *Hiawatha* (10)
5. Opposite of 'out' (2)
6. Slang food (4)
7. It's white in winter (4)
12. Small insect (3)
13. The opposite of beginning (3)
14. Rub the tongue over something (4)
15. River that flows through Paris (5)
17. Abbreviated Automobile Association (2)
19. Initials at the end of geometry theorems (3)
21. Reject someone you love (4)
24. Utilise (3)
26. Different—in an odd sort of way (9)
27. ICE BOD—Old-fashioned garment (6)
28. Famous school that sounds as if it has been swallowed (4)
29. The cat sat on it (3)
32. Striking implement used in cricket (3)
35. To take what is given (6)
36. Short thanks (2)
38. Joins your head to your shoulders (4)
40. To work things out intelligently (6)
41. Rear end of a ship (5)
43. Used by fishermen (3)
46. Short hire purchase (2)
47. French the (2)
The answers are on page 128

Beat Your Teacher at Arithmetic

Ask your arithmetic teacher to write down any five-digit number. As an example we will assume he has written down 63,851.

Underneath this, *you* write down a five-digit number. It should look as if you are writing this at random. What you are really doing is putting down the difference between his numbers and the number 9. So, in the example just mentioned (when the teacher put down 63,851) you will write down 36,148.

Now ask the teacher to write down another line of numbers and you do the same. Again, all you have to do is to write down the differences between his digits and the number 9. Let us assume that the third line written down by your teacher is 56,029—you therefore have written 43,970.

You now have four rows of figures. Ask your teacher to write down another row. Immediately he has done this you draw a line beneath the five rows, and, faster than your teacher can do it, add up all the figures in your head.

What your teacher will not realise is that there is a trick to this rapid calculation. In actual fact you can do the adding up quite easily. To add up the five rows quickly, all you have to do is to look at the last five-figure number written down by your teacher. Take 2 away from the last digit and write down a 2 in front of the remaining digits. So, if your teacher writes down 73,938 for the fifth number your answer to the whole sum will be 273,936.

Here is another example to show you the whole sum. You will see that the first (written by the teacher) and the second row (written by you) add up to 9 as do the fourth and fifth rows.

$$
\begin{array}{r}
32,491 \\
67,508 \\
74,215 \\
25,784 \\
87,592 \\
\hline
287,590
\end{array}
$$

The last row (written by the teacher) in this example is 87,592, so all you do is take away 2 to give 87,590 and then put a 2 in front of the figures to give you the answer 287,590. If you do not believe this, add up the five rows and you will see that the answer is correct.

Be Someone Who Counts

According to the dictionary, a billion is a million million. When written down it looks like this:

1,000,000,000,000

Quite an ordinary number, you may think, so how long do you think it would take to you to count from one to a billion? You can try it if you like but you will find that even at your fastest you can count only up to about two hundred in one minute. At this rate, assuming you could keep it up for you would not be able to stop for food, drink, sleep, school, or television, it would take you at least 9,512 years before you reached a billion.

In America and France a billion is only a thousand million, 1,000,000,000, but even that would take you something like ten years to count.

Both of these calculations have ignored leap years which will help to reduce the time only by a few years, or, with the American billion, only a few days.

Classroom Shooter

There are several skills that should be in the repertoire of every Whizzkid. One of them is the ability to shoot elastic bands across the classroom. This is how it is done:

Put one end of a thin elastic band over the tip of your forefinger. Now take the band over your thumb and hook the other end over your little finger. Second and third fingers should be folded into the palm to keep them out of the way.

Point your forefinger at the target and lift your little finger to release the elastic band. It will shoot across the room, straight towards your target and, with a bit of luck, hit him on the back of the neck!

The more you can stretch the band with the little finger the faster and the further it will go when released. With practice an enterprising Whizzkid should be able to fire an elastic band from each hand at the same time.

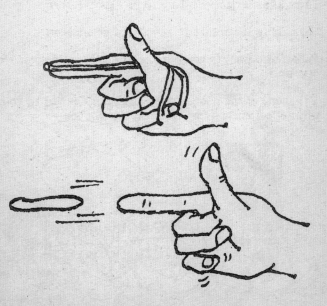

Careers Advice

Games for the School Bus

If you want to be a flea trainer when you leave school, you'll have to be prepared to start from scratch.

An astronaut's job is really out of this world.

If you want to be a roaring success, become a lion tamer.

If you become a baker you'll always make plenty of dough.

An oil driller's work is boring.

To be a human canonball you *must* be a person of the right calibre—and willing to travel.

If people regard you as a drop-out you might be successful as a parachutist.

To be a lumberjack you have to be a decent feller.

For a job you can stick to—become a glue-maker.

People who want to go up in the world should become lift operators.

(If none of the above career suggestions appeal to you, why not become a sweep—that should soot you.)

Games for the School Bus

It is sometimes boring travelling on the school bus (especially *going* to school) so here are a few games that will help to make that boring but essential journey a little more enjoyable.

FUNNY PHRASES

This is best played at the back of the bus. Look out of the rear window and see who can make the funniest phrase out of the letters of the vehicle that is travelling immediately behind the bus. Ignore the numbers, you'll find it difficult to make phrases out of them.

Let us suppose that you see the number SDL334T. Ignore the numbers and the suffix letter and just use SDL which you can make into Sausages Drink Lemonade, or Sidney's Dog Limps . . . well, I'm sure you can come up with something funnier than that.

If the letters are FJH you could make Fleas Jump Heartily or Fresh Jellied Hippopotamus or Flying Jazz Harpists.

To make sure there are no, or at least not many, arguments as to who has made up the funniest or the wittiest phrases you should appoint a member of the back seat gang to act as judge.

CRAZY CROSSWORDS

Each player has to first draw a grid of twenty-five squares

in a block five squares by five. The first person calls out a letter of the alphabet and each player (including the one who called the letter) writes it down in one of the squares on his grid. The letter can be placed anywhere but some skill, and possibly cunning, should be used to work out what will be the best position for that letter.

The players then take it in turns to call out a letter which everyone writes on his or her grid. At the end of the game, when each player has called the same number of letters, the players count up to see how many complete words each person has scored. The person with the most words is of course the winner.

Much of the skill and luck of this game depends upon the positioning of the letters called out by the other players. When it is your turn you, of course, call out a letter that will help you to form the words that you are trying to get.

↓ REMEMBER
TO SELECT A JUDGE

MATHS MASTERMIND

This game was devised by a sadistic arithmetic teacher so his pupils could practise their multiplication tables. It can however make a good game to play on the school bus— provided that the maths master is not around to hear how brilliant, or dim, you really are.

One person calls out the numbers from a car registration plate and each player has to multiply the numbers together and come up with an answer. So if the car number is LTF252M the two and the five are multiplied to make ten and this is then multiplied by two to make twenty (notice how the author picks easy examples? They're the only ones he can do!)

The only problem with this game is working out who has won. When you have five players and you get five different answers, the person selected as the judge has quite a problem on his hands.

GESTAPO GAME

One person is selected as the victim and all the other players are Gestapo Agents. The Gestapo fire questions at the victim as fast as they can. The victim has to answer each question as rapidly as he can but he must not use the replies "yes," "no", or "I don't know". If he uses any of these replies he is out and someone else is selected as the victim.

See how long you can survive under such intensive questioning—it is not so easy as you may think.

SCHOOL SAUSAGES AND CHIPS

This is an old favourite but it is still good enough to produce roars of laughter on the school bus. One person is selected as the school canteen supervisor. The rest of the players are customers of the school canteen and they have to ask the supervisor questions. To each question the supervisor must answer what all school canteen supervisors reply when you ask them a question, "Sausages and Chips".

So the conversation may proceed along the following lines:

What do you put in your school books?
Sausages and chips.
Who is your form teacher?
Sausages and chips.
What lies across the Irish Sea?
Sausages and chips.

And so it continues until the supervisor laughs or even smiles. As soon as he does so he has to resign and another supervisor has to be appointed.

Be Top at Languages

The learning of foreign language vocabulary at school can be made a lot easier if you first observe the similarities between English and the language being learned. Some words are exactly the same in the foreign language as they are in English, although of course the pronunciation is different. Just look at these examples from French and you will get some idea of how many words are really easy to learn.

ENGLISH	FRENCH
biscuit	le biscuit
blouse	la blouse
bracelet	le bracelet
centre	le centre
certain	certain
chance	la chance
direction	la direction
distance	la distance
garage	le garage
guide	le guide
message	le message
million	le million
nature	la nature
police	la police
possible	possible
sauce	la sauce
simple	simple
table	la table
train	le train
vase	le vase
village	le village
voyage	le voyage
zero	le zero

These examples were chosen at random and you will find many many more if you care to look for them. The same principle works with other languages. Here are a few from German:

ENGLISH	GERMAN
arm	der Arm
butter	die Butter
drama	das Drama
finger	der Finger
hand	die Hand
hunger	der Hunger
land	das Land
museum	das Museum
post	die Post
problem	das Problem
restaurant	das Restaurant
September	der September
sofa	das Sofa
station	die Station
student	der Student
tourist	der Tourist
warm	warm
wind	der Wind
winter	der Winter

And, again, this does not exhaust the list of words that are the same in each language. So now you can see how easy it is to learn another language. But the Whizzkid does not stop there. When he has learned the words that are the same he realises that there are many words that are so similar; they, too, are extremely easy to learn. In French, these words include the following:

ENGLISH	FRENCH
to accuse	accuser
actor	l'acteur
banana	la banane
brief	bref
butcher	le boucher
calm	calme
cat	le chat
chocolate	le chocolat
colour	le coleur
to continue	continuer
lemonade	la limonade
letter	la lettre
list	la liste
November	Novembre
ordinary	ordinaire
salad	la salade
tomato	le tomate

In German, the similar words include the following:

ENGLISH	GERMAN
book	das Buch
clear	klar
cool	kühl
end	das Ende
friend	der Freund
glass	das Glas
here	hier
to kiss	küssen
milk	die Milch
new	neu
passenger	der Passagier
place	der Platz
price	der Preis
school	die Schule
shoe	der Schuh
when	wenn

See how many more you can find. And when you have found as many as you can you will have quite an extensive foreign vocabulary. There is, however, an easy way of learning even more words and that is to learn those that, although not the same or even similar, do have a connection with the English language. All you have to do is think of the connecting word and that will give you a clue as to what the word is in the language you are studying. Here are some examples:

ENGLISH	Connecting Word	FRENCH
answer	response	la réponse
brave	courageous	courageux
busy	occupied	occupé
dish	plate	le plat
end	finish	la fin
famous	celebrity	célèbre
genuine	authentic	authentique
hundred	century	cent
hunger	famished	la faim
joke	pleasant	la plaisanterie
light	illuminate	la lumière
passenger	voyage	le voyageur
room	chamber	la chambre
seldom	rare	rarement
sick	malady	malade
strange	curious	curieux
tooth	dentist	le dent

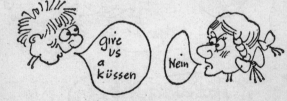

And in German:

ENGLISH	Connecting Word	GERMAN
cake	cooking	der Kuchen
car	waggon	der Wagen
chair	stool	der Stuhl
clock	hour	die Uhr
factory	fabricate	die Fabrik
flower	bloom	die Blume
forest	wold	der Wald
girl	maiden	das Mädchen
glove	hand shoe	der Handshuh
goods	wares	die Ware
ink	tint	die Tinte
lady	dame	die Dame
noise	alarm	der Lärm
to buy petrol	petrol tank	tanken
rule	regular	die Regel
to teach	learn	lehren
ticket	card	die Karte

It is even possible to use these similarities of language to learn words from several languages simultaneously. Just take a look at the list below and you will get some idea of how easy it can be.

ENGLISH	FRENCH	GERMAN
automobile	l'automobile	das Automobil
ball	la balle	der Ball
class	la classe	die Klasse
coffee	le café	der Kaffee
concert	le concert	das Konzert
family	la famille	die Familie
fresh	frais	frisch
garden	le jardin	der Garten
hotel	l'hôtel	das Hotel
intelligent	intelligent	intelligent
interesting	intéressant	interessant
lamp	la lampe	die Lampe
long	long	lang
market	le marché	der Markt
minute	la minute	die Minute
music	la musique	die Musik
naturally	naturellement	natürlich
paper	le papier	das Papier
park	le parc	der Park
person	la personne	die Person
photograph	la photographie	die Photographie
portrait	le portrait	das Porträt
professor	le professeur	der Professor
programme	le programme	das Programm
radio	le radio	das Radio
soup	la soupe	die Suppe
sum	la somme	die Summe
taxi	le taxi	das Taxi
tea	le thé	der Tee
telephone	le téléphone	das Telephon
theatre	le thèâtre	das Theater
uncle	l'oncle	der Onkel

And there you are! If you go through the words on the previous pages a couple of times it will not take very long to learn them all. And you will then know 89 French words and 84 German words. Look through your language dictionaries for other similar words and it will not be long before you are top of the class in languages!

School Library

Here is a selection of books that should be found in most school libraries:

LET X EQUAL Y by Al G. Brar
FOREST COLOURS by Theresa Green
CAKE DECORATIONS by I. Sing
HOW TO MILK A COW (in ten squeezy lessons)
  by Ivor Stool
AVOIDING TRAFFIC JAMS by Dai Version
FURTHER EDUCATION by Una Versity

Biology Baffler

In a biology exam the pupils were asked to draw a picture of an amoeba, one of the simplest forms of life. The correct drawing is shown here. Below are the attempts of nine examinees to draw the same thing. Of the nine attempts, only one is exactly right. Which one is it?

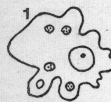

1

2

3

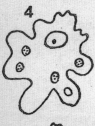

4

5

6

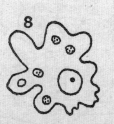

7

8

9

The answer is on page 128.

Answers to Puzzles

LESSON TIMETABLE

The first lesson of the day is Chemistry. This is followed by Biology, Geography, and then Arithmetic. The pupils then take a lunch break after which they have English, French, History and Physics.

COCK-EYED COUNTRIES

Australia; United States of America; South America; New Zealand; India.

CLASSROOM CHANGES

In the bottom picture there is an 'S' in 'DETENTIONS'; the third line of writing on the wall is different; there is one less stud on the door; the teacher's mortar board is different; the cane has an extra joint; the crack in the ceiling is bigger; there is one more dot round the window; the rope noose is different; the paper on the right-hand desk is bigger; there is a pen in the inkwell in the bottom right-hand corner.

HIDDEN LESSONS

Algebra; Arithmetic; Art; Biology; Chemistry; English; French; Geography; Geometry; History; Music; Physics.

WHO TEACHES WHAT?

A = Sammy Colon; B = Brad Awl; C = 'Nosey' Parker; D = 'Spud' Murphy; E = Ivor Grudge; F = Mark Time; G = Jim Nasium.

IN THE PICTURE

In the bottom picture the eye of the boy on the far left is different; the boy to his right has no cuff, and his tie is shorter; the boy with a bow tie has a black button on his shirt; the tassel on the teacher's mortar board is bigger; the boy in the front row, third from the right, has a different mouth; the boy on his right has a shorter nose; the boy on the far right has shorter hair and his tie has a black stripe; the eye of a boy on the teacher's right is different.

WHICH SCHOOL?

1. Lowood; 2. St. Trinians; 3. Greyfriars; 4. Eton; 5. St. Custards; 6. Rugby; 7. Gordonstoun; 8. Dotheboys Hall; 9. Harrow.

WHIZZKID'S CROSSWORD

Across: 1. Mime; 4. Latin; 8. OK; 9. Solo; 10. Noon; 11. Neat; 13. English; 16. Titan; 18. Fi; 20. Adjective; 22. Ilk; 23. Du; 25. Ye; 27. Bell; 29. Me; 30. Otto; 31. OBE; 33. Do; 34. Watt; 37. Inn; 39. Art; 42. Stretcher; 44. Act; 45. Pots; 47. Ltd; 48. Scapula; 49. Anon.

Down: 1. Monotony; 2. Ike; 3. Est; 4. Longfellow; 5. In; 6. Nosh; 7. Snow; 12. Ant; 13. End; 14. Lick; 15. Seine; 17. AA; 19. QED; 21. Jilt; 24. Use; 26. Eccentric; 27. Bodice; 28. Eton; 29. Mat; 32. Bat; 35. Accept; 36. Ta; 38. Neck; 40. Reason; 41. Stern; 43. Rod; 46. HP; 47. La.

BIOLOGY BAFFLER

No. 8 is the same.